APOSTROPHES II   through you I

APOSTROPHES II

through you I
E.D. Blodgett

The University of Alberta Press

First published by
    The University of Alberta Press
    141 Athabasca Hall
    Edmonton, Alberta, Canada T6G 2E8

Apostrophes II: through you I is a publication for the book trade from the University of Alberta Press.

Printed in Canada 5 4 3 2
Copyright © E.D. Blodgett 1997
ISBN 0–88864–304–7

Canadian Cataloguing in Publication Data

Blodgett, E. D. (Edward Dickinson), 1935–
    Apostrophes II

Poems.
ISBN 0–88864–304–7

    1. Title.
PS8553.L56A67 1997   C811'.54   C97–911106–4
PR9199.3.B54A67 1997

A volume in (*cuRRents*), an interdisciplinary series. Jonathan Hart, series editor.

All rights reserved.

No part of this publication may be produced, stored in a retrieval system, or transmitted in any form or by any means, electronic, mechanical, photocopying, recording, or otherwise, without the prior permission of the copyright owner.

Printed and bound in Canada by Friesens, Altona, Manitoba.
∞ Printed on acid-free paper.

The University of Alberta Press gratefully acknowledges the support received for its publishing program from the Canada Council for the Arts, the Department of Canadian Heritage, and the Alberta Foundation for the Arts.

  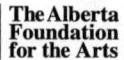  

COMMITTED TO THE DEVELOPMENT OF CULTURE AND THE ARTS

Por ti soy imagen, por ti soy otro, por ti soy.

Octavio Paz

Senti? Questi è la voce
che non l'orecchio intende
ma il trasalire solo del tuo silenzio
dedito al sogno celeste della musica.

Arturo Onofri

Tibi

Contents

- 9 Outside
- 10 Awake
- 11 *Carole*
- 12 Measures
- 13 Prayers
- 14 Revisions
- 15 Blind
- 16 Sites
- 17 Adrift
- 18 Nocturne
- 19 Witness
- 20 Alchemy
- 21 Exchanging
- 22 Translation
- 23 Adagia
- 24 First Light
- 25 Synthesis
- 26 Transcription
- 27 Disclosures
- 28 Evensong
- 29 Doorways
- 30 Epigraph
- 31 Nightfall
- 32 Attendance
- 33 Dead Reckoning
- 34 Opening
- 35 Little Song
- 36 Sunbathing
- 37 Play
- 38 Correspondence
- 39 Eclipse
- 40 Toccata
- 41 Implications
- 42 Voice
- 43 Apocalypse
- 44 Sleeping
- 45 Vigils
- 46 Departures
- 47 Passages
- 48 Waking
- 49 Refractions
- 50 Crows
- 51 Rogation
- 52 Gifts
- 53 *Clair de Lune*
- 54 Obbligato
- 55 Logos
- 56 *Essai*
- 57 Breath
- 58 Epigram
- 59 Acacias
- 60 Imago
- 61 Vocation
- 62 Parting
- 63 Moonrise
- 64 Harvest
- 65 Rondel
- 66 Waiting
- 67 Absence
- 68 Zenith
- 69 Speaking
- 70 Reply
- 71 Of Roses
- 72 Palingenesis
- 73 Naked
- 74 Returned

Outside

I saw you naked on the grass. No stone would lie
so, the winds of planets falling on your flesh. I could not tell
if this were birth or death, to see the moon upon your skin, to know
the emptiness of air. What am I now to do, possessing such
a solitude, the weight of nothing in my hands? What if rain
should fall on you, then the night, and you a little dark for me
to stumble on, a random thing within the world? I do not wish

to move my hands, to see the absence they disturb. Nowhere can
we walk but into possibility. I kneel beside you on
the grass, entering the nakedness of wind and flesh and dark.
Nothing can be helped, not even grass, and knowing is no more
than this abandoning of birth and death, no other certitudes
of sun and moon, both of us lying here, waiting for
the wind, a change of rain, the patient temporalities of grass.

Awake

You woke. The space around your body gathers in the light. Beneath
the planets, small explosions of the birds appear, the air turned
to music in the light. I could not see you for the roses that
blew beneath the birds. You smell of sleep, you said, your voice within
a cosmos speaking. How should I reply now, uncertain of
what you are, of air and bird and rose? If I could see your eyes,

their fragrance from your sleeping might come over me, a fall of light
upon my flesh. I shall not know if this has any name, the dawn
you have become, a world rising up within my eyes. What are
we, then, but beings in our breath, uttering our sun and moon
that lie inside us when we sleep—their sweetness layers in our bones,
planets give us shape, the music of our breath awake with light.

Carole

The world lies beside you sleeping in its silence. Even the moon,
following the setting sun, encloses you within its grave
embrace, rituals of planets passing round your head. I think
that when you wake, you will become a space, and all that anyone
will see is your turning there. Silence, when I touch it, flows
upon my skin. It is not you, but old possessions of the moon that is

what we become, passing through the night, a universe within
its autumns, stars falling. Nothing that might have been my flesh is mine.
What are we now, knowing such an ecstasy? Whenever tides
will flow against our feet, a recognition will befall us—: this
is where we were when we were young, light descending on us from
the moon, our knowing then the dance of gravity that enters us.

Measures

Tell me of the absoluteness of the night the moon began
to shape its solitude within your eyes, the moon's silence now
yours, your flesh steeped. When I touch your face, a universe
enters me, wherever planets, stars and moon have moved. The dark
has died. How shall I begin to tell the shape your life takes
now, measures of the light unstrung? Where shall I find the place

where it began, a primal word spoken that possesses all
other words, original finality suspended in
the ancient night? Telling of mutations of the moon is what
we speak, each word declining into night. The moon is not
of stone, the moon is how you enter air, face space, take all
beginning in, and bear away tidings of mortality.

Prayers

As others say their prayers, we would tell each other stories in
the dark, and they would reach around us till within their arms we fell
asleep. We spoke of us as flesh and its becoming word, the light
that enters us the light of our speaking, bones that gather in
the fire dancing through the quick economy of our breath,
the voices of our body turning through itself. We spoke of you
and me, both of us persona of ourself, this trinity

that we surrender to our words. It seems that when we speak that we
are born of silence, our origin an exhalation of
the you and me that are suspended in our mouths. We did not learn
this anywhere but here, the language that we know a speech of flesh,
the dark, the breath where we are shaped. Silence wraps around us when
we fall asleep, no other memory of us to be heard. We sleep
inside ourself, our birth a breath away, asleep upon our tongues.

Revisions

I caught myself standing at a window, my gaze going through
the trees, the shapes of light around them broken by branch and leaf,
and finally through the light, nothing appearing in my eyes, the sun
turning alone within another universe. I do not want
to look upon recessions of eternity, a flower growing
backward through its seed, nothing but the ground to see. You died

too soon, my friend, and when I wish to speak, to tell you of the light,
words but barely born die before they reach my tongue, a mouth
possessed of silences. There the sun within its solitudes
would pass, the winds within their emptiness. The space of galaxies,
is nowhere, friend, but settled in our flesh. Stars unhoused fall
nightly there, gravities of darkness slip slowly forth.

Blind

The world beneath the sun cannot be known. I give it up—the name
of absolutes unshadowed in the mind. When you enter me,
you bring the night within your hand, its opening a gift. What can
I do, believing I am blind, but take your hand to draw the dark
more carefully around us where we lie, knowing you within
my grasp? Birds pass through the night. Memories sound so, falling
into night. Should I look, it would be only in your eyes,

to touch what light there is with mine. Perhaps the moon within your night
might flower from the garden of the sky, the light in its largesse
filling us. I know your eyes when mine consider yours, your hand
when it has touched mine. How do we live within each other's eyes,
the moon possessing us? We are not made to know. Wherever in
the dark you are, the moon within its tropics turns—: if it could
be held, fate, the falling stars, would find an orbit in your hand.

Sites

Birds were standing on your shoulders, music and the moon rising
in the air, and where you walked, flowers were awake. There are
no consequences here, the heavens and the stars remain unchanged,
but bright, bright upon your face the moon reflected on itself,
light in converse with the birds. You think of grass, the infinite
refrains of birds, their slow turns of thought within the dark, the moon's
mortality immortal in your eyes. Somewhere tides must come

to mind, music rippling through the air, coasts unknown that rise
above the sea. I cannot tell the place, somewhere between the moon
and fragments of the moon above the wave, birds making light
of night, nor can I say how into these reflections I have stepped,
recalling grass, the flowers in your wake, the shade I cast upon
the sea floating randomly away. To be your thinking me
is where I am, water music plays there, beneath the moon.

Adrift

The trees became shade and entered our eyes, the liquid dark
descending in our flesh. Beside us in the stream, the moon lay
at rest, a moon of glass and water flowing blue beneath. You might
have thought it was divinity absorbed within its gaze, the moon
reflecting on another moon. Nothing lay upon our skin
but silence, shade and air rising blue. You moved your hand to touch
the floating moon, water falling from your hands around us through

the air, fragments of the moon enclosing us. Could it be
that when the moment of apocalypse occurs, the moon will fall
apart, its mysteries revealed, the light flowing blue against
our flesh? Everything flows forever—moons, streams, the dark—
this is to stand within the moon, all its phases flowing and
nothing here to hold but water and ourselves, where fountains of
the light splash through our flesh, immortality adrift.

Nocturne

It must have been crows I heard, entering their distances,
bearing over the flowered earth brief songs of death within
their mouths. I cannot tell you where they were, perhaps inside the mind
alone, memories turning dark, vesper crows that call against
the sun. Twilight enters us, uncertain what our speaking means,
roses sometimes leaping from our mouths, gardens taking shape
upon our lips. The silence after crows have passed does not

relieve the air. No one will bear the earth away when it
will cease to turn, nor the sun unmoving hanging in
the air, nothing to do, nor distances that fill our eyes, nor stars
in their descents, nor any word we spoke. Is it possible,
beneath the shades that gather in the dark, the air scored for crows,
to hear roses open in the silence, gravity flower and
the moon, the night at home within our flesh, no other place to go?

Witness

You said the other night I passed into your dream. Gravity
became a singing bird, aloft within the firmament. All
volition in my body disappeared. I cannot say how long
I gazed upon my hands, seeing them as they opened, both a rose
and I their earth, clouds above and clouds beneath. No longer could
I stroke the air, but music hovered there between the clouds and where

I was, the birds prismatic in the light, the music passing through
my eyes. What might the sun be now, somewhere solitary in
your dream, everything I see possessed of its fugacity?
The words I might have spoken lose themselves in air. Perhaps they have
become birds, each one departing from the darkness of
my flesh, as roses of my hands exhale the silence into light.

Alchemy

I felt your bones beneath your flesh. The trees within their weathers are
no more patient than your bones could be. Perhaps there are birds
that dwell within the mind, unimaginable birds that sit
through all the seasons on your bones. I think that at the moment of
apocalypse, when bones stand up and sing, it will be birds like these,
birds none can see, that shall take wing invisibly and leap

upward to the sun, to utter one by one the silence that
they keep, the sun taking in their words, becoming slowly white
and fading into space, the patience of our bones, the dust that drifts
within the universe, a cosmos then anatomized. I felt
your bones—: the sun in its fragilities is at my finger tips,
a transmutation of the birds, our flesh the only music known.

Exchanging

You breathed upon my face. Is this what Adam felt, his body still
smelling of the earth, the newly made roots, the grass within
its first season, rain and sun, when God in his exhaling filled
his flesh? And I inhaled—the grass, a sense of sun transmuting us.
Everywhere the air was changed when Adam spoke, trees stood still,
the birds surprised and beasts. It was not music spoken nor lament,

but something of the earth and something of another's air. If we
can utter holiness, it would be nowhere else but here, within
the space of syllables that flow over from your mouth to fill
the earth of mine, mortalities exchanged within the air. The flesh
I think I am is where the beasts return at night. The moon appears,
and shadows that our shapes assume are grass within our mouth.

Translation

You drew yourself above us—everything, the trees, the barest fall
of rain, traces of music birds abandon in the air, the sun
possessed of April light—and both of us stretched forth our hands in one
insistence, hands entering the air. I look upon your hands
to see the sun in its transfusions passing through your bones. When
the sun ascends, it rises first within the mind, a light invisible

that forms, and all around it passages of birds, sudden stars
in jubilation. Beneath this sun you first began to move,
figuring the light, the sun drawn into your wake. I sit
within the other tropics of the light. The grass against my feet
appears to open, silence, green, the rain. The sun is smaller there—:
take it in your hands. There is no other light for us to know.

Adagia

The rain in freshets fell upon our bodies, raining in our mouths,
our eyes, the hollows of our knees. I turned to touch your cheeks and smelled
the grass already growing on them, violets and smaller lilies
of the field. When the sun rose, the light was not as it
had been, it was a second skin where beasts within the morning drink,
going round, moving with the pace the planets use. It was
not possible to see the stars, but when the dark was spread across

our flesh, the distance of the light began to settle in us. If I
could speak, my words would be a movement of the air within the trees,
a circularity of birds. Why did we think that we were never
so, imagining we moved, imagining we thought? There are
rainy reaches of the mind, and if we were to dance, a dance
of fern and moss and other measures of the grass, we could not think
otherwise, abandoned to the rain, wisdom falling we thought

against our feet, against the ground. I smell again the grass that grows
from somewhere in your flesh, inhaling sapience and rain, the earth
within you going round, the light becoming green. No other dance
can comprehend the movement that they make, the earth illumined and
the grass. Wisdom is the space we cannot see that comes before
the rain——: we know it falling through us, raining through the darkness and
entering us. The grass we are is gnomic, it kneels before light.

First Light

When you awoke, the light within the room changed. I heard the birds
that until then were silent. Tides began to rise and fall. I reached
to take you in my arms, to grasp the sun flowing from your flesh—:
I touched your head, your arms, your back at random. Sometimes I think you are
the grass, or trees before their leaves have come, radiant within
the sun. What if we spoke? What would the figures mean reflecting from you,

aspects of the light? I see I must begin in silence. If
knowing is the sun, belief falls from the moon. This must be
the sense of tides, the rhythms that I make learning how to speak
to you. The world is only known in pieces, grasses, tides and suns,
word by word. All night I lay beside you, breathing as
you breathed, oceans moving through me, shades of islands rising at dawn.

Synthesis

We stood among the trees, the shades of leaves falling on our skin.
Sometimes there were birds to hear, ghosting through the air. I think
we cannot see the sun, nor discern the phases of the moon.
All we are to know is in our flesh, the songs we heard, the earth
against our feet where smaller creatures ran, the presence of the trees.
The sun is warm upon our skin, against the cooler patches of
the shade. What kind of summa might this be? Beneath the light trees

breathe with no more sound than we, and as they breathe, leaves appear,
open and fall, holding the sun a little while, becoming shade.
No one ever spoke with trees, but they are in us, mortality
and shade, and in us are the slow migrations of the birds that bear
polar tropics to our core. I cannot think of meanings in
the stars, nothing but the earth, its darkness our form, to know
within us, other immediacies of the sun taking root.

Transcription

We stood within the circle of the sun. The days did not dissolve
into the night, but turned upon themselves. Gravity, perhaps,
does not avail, and looking in your eyes, eternity did not
appear invisible, but paleographies of stars arose.
We could be no more naked and alone. Should the wind descend
upon us, we would bend beneath its force. Apocalypse is more,

but only liminal. Were I to tell you of my death, I would
not give the day, but standing so, becoming rose, how can we know
of sun and star? The light is everywhere, and as we open, shades
disperse. Why did I think myself mere bone and flesh, a thing where light
and air give way? The sun does not ascend against the sky, it is
the rose of our rising, endless tropology within the light.

Disclosures

You said the roses now have opened, and we saw it was not they
alone that opened, but the air that we were breathing seemed to lie
in layers in our mouths. Nor do I think that we could see the sun
suspended in its absence——: we saw the instances of bees, a sun
in fragments leaping through the air. If any rain fell, its fall

was interstitial. We thought that we could lie upon the ground,
to feel the grass begin to enter us, but where we saw the earth
was roses in their opening, fragilities of air and rain.
All of this was what we were inhaling, roses expectant in
our flesh, not us moving now but bees, exfoliating sun.

Evensong

You sat upon the stairs. There were flowers in your hand. Sunlight fell
across your face. You moved to place the flowers in my hand, and so
I sat beside you, economies of silence filling us, neither
sleeping nor awake, two birds within a flowering tree
open between the earth and sky. A world without a past is such
a place, no one sure of any shape it has. Music comes

upon us then, a music binding earth and sky. Paradise,
perhaps, is nothing else, and when I spoke within the silence of
the flowers that you held, I was no longer certain of the stairs
beneath us, whether they rose or fell. The words I spoke invisibly
take shape around us, a garden in its summer. I give them to you one
by one, to hear the setting sun sound its nocturnes in your ear.

Doorways

You stood unmoving in the doorway asking, are we remembered when
we die, or smells of lilac briefly passing, or the rain that falls
through each successive spring? I looked into your eyes and saw them closed,
a silence spilling from them on your face, nor could I place my hand
at any moment into yours without the comprehension of
the silence sheathing us. And when I die, where will I be when you

remember me? We do not live in place, my friend, standing here
between a sun and moon, but in the time that lives in us. We breathe
each other's breath in time, the rhythm of our temporality
exchanged: remembering the rain we are transformed. I cannot say
whose silence spreads across your face, what other passages that you
have known, other lilacs that descend at random into time.

Epigraph

I think of you beneath large trees. Beside you is a stream
flowing down beneath the trees. Nothing is seen above it but
stones, and sometimes a fallen leaf. No one knows whether the sun
or moon has ever entered here beneath the trees, and if you raised
your hands, darkness would settle there, and you might think it was a bird,
a darkness edged with fear and still warm. I never saw your eyes,

nor where their gaze would disappear, deeper in the trees. But most
of all it is your speaking that I hear, eternities of words
mounting against the dark, the flowers when you spoke growing old,
and grass. Someday a stream will flow forever through your flesh, the dark
illumined with other flowers breathing, turned beneath finalities
of trees toward your mouth. Your hands will open. Birds will leap apart.

Nightfall

You sat within the firelight, alone, the light falling on
your shoulder through the dark. The room fell apart into shade,
nor was it possible to tell if chairs or walls were anywhere
nearby. Perhaps only air is left, an air that proffers to
our hands the space through which a planet moves. Only your shoulder seems
to keep a memory of who we are or might have been. I fear

that should I touch it, my hand grazing through the dark, that something of
the dust that planets leave might settle there. Solitude is not
an absence but a shift within the light, a loss of something known,
things falling out of place and through the dark. Our voices drift,
no one able to say where they are coming from—perhaps the air. Nothing
rises from your shoulder, neither grass nor tree, except the stars.

Attendance

The words you spoke settled on your lips. Flowers appeared and grass,
trees and the small stones, rising in your breath. Animals
were standing in the shade, your breathing in their flesh. The memory
of earth is of the air alone, brief afflatus rising from nowhere
known, a crown of stars upon her head. What is there for the earth
to do, waiting upon the silence of the sun and uttering
the grass? Never was the logos made of flesh, but palpable

the sun comes up in every flower. We arise from earth, and when
you speak, the fragrance of a resurrection emanating from
your mouth, it is an earth translated in your breath that floats between
us here. I sit with darkness everywhere, waiting for you to speak
me, the longing of the sun become a cosmos listening,
a knowledge of the muteness of the grass springing up before
my eyes, to be the word you speak, your breathing through my being gone.

Dead Reckoning

Now that death has entered you, sooner than I think it will
arrive in me, I fear to look into your eyes and see the sun
growing dimmer there. The space around my hands, unable to
contain the stars, begins to fail. Who would have thought that not the air
alone but space itself would die, the planets disappearing and
the seasons smaller? Between us on a table flowers floated in

a bowl. Flowers, you said, are flowers forever, each coming back
within the next. You gazed into the bowl and looked away, and when
your eyes returned, I looked to see in each the image of a rose
reflecting on mortality. There must be moments when we are
uncertain where we are, the sun beyond our measure, being seen,
after it is gone, mirage of roses passing through the sky.

Opening

We were making love. I saw the muscles of your face grow taut beneath your skin. I gazed into your eyes and saw a vestige of myself, a setting sun. If I should speak now, who would speak and who would hear? For us the world fell away on either side—: we may have been somewhere else, forgotten and alone, and were we seen, there would not be a thing to see, impossible to sculpt. Flowers, when they open, change the silence of the air, and all

interrogation ends, an overture of roses rising beneath the sun, and each a sentence that affirms the rose in its invisibility. We need not, then, be known. But to unfold— silence in its flower, manifold articulation of the air—this is how we have been chosen to become, the rose forever rose. The light I see that passes through your eyes does not grow dark, it changes key, rosaria that flowers in our flesh.

Little Song

We stopped at land's end, your hand in mine, facing the sea. There was
a mist above the waves where now and then a boat emerged, surprised
by light. I do not recall the sounds of birds, only the fall of waves
against our feet, the gasp of their return. It did not seem as if
the sea could ever lose an aspect of itself, the land alone
wearing down——: the trees and stones that stood about were tended by
the sea, and in the end they enter there, becoming sea and cloud

and rain. We are permitted, then, to stand here, your hand in mine,
sharing stillness with the stones, the unremitting rhythms of
the sea already entering our flesh. You said that when you die,
you would not ask for roses, no illusion of eternity
to stand beside you in a vase. Your wish was this, that music would
wash over you, a music larger than the sea, the patience of
the merest stone surging up at last in jubilant refrain.

Sunbathing

We did not know how we had reached this place, but waited for the tide,
knowing the moon aloft within the music of the sea. Upon
the shore there lay fossils of fish, the absence of their bones inscribed
on stone, a sense of music after it has gone. We could not help
but sense the trees behind us somewhere in their immobility,
dreaming the sun that comes and goes around them, dancing on their leaves,
their branches stretching through the air anatomized. We did not stoop

to touch the signs of fish, their memories of moons that moved them up
and down the coasts, fearing sudden dissolution in our hands.
I placed my hand upon your back, the warmth of flesh composing us
in low relief between the sea and trees. Our bones cannot be ours,
dwelling only briefly in our flesh, the bones we take to be
in our grasp a harvest for the sun, and we but instants of
the light that plays upon the moon and sea, the air etched.

Play

Barely awake beneath the sun, your voice began to rise within
the air. We thought it might have been a bird, the song you sang, or star
or moon within its phases moving through the trees, but when we looked,
we saw that what it was had gone, a cosmos in its signs departing
from us. I could not move, abandoned to the music taking shape
again within my flesh, a dance unknown to me, no moon, but light,
no trees but silence there where I had been. I reached to touch your face,

to take, perhaps, the words that flowered from your mouth, but no hand
answered my desire, nothing but a play of light within
the stillness moving me, a willow in the sun, unable to
behold the air, but knowing other trees, the fleshing of the world.
We cannot help ourselves—star, willow, bird—poised between
the sun and moon, a gravity that grows beneath us, even through
the grass, the air of our breathing turning round a universe.

Correspondence

I did not see the stars within your eyes but saw them turning round
your body, naked as another planet resting in the air.
What else will be more absolute than this, no other scene to gauge
you by but stars and space receding farther than the thought of it,
space dissolving into silence, you the shape it takes, your flesh
in some archaic speech articulating alphabets that we
decipher through the darkness of returning nights, your lifted hand

lyric enough? Why stop for roses, eyes, the bones I know
more than mine, when streams, the trees in their economies emerge
forever through your flesh, each becoming word among the stars?
Should someone ask, who shall I say you are, and where you lie among
the other turning spheres, their music falling over yours, a rain
of music playing on your tongue, enigmas housing there, bereft
of all response but letters of our being written in the air?

Eclipse

You stood against the sun, your eyes becoming full of shadowed time. There is
no exit from this place. The night your body is—the distances
of stars, versions of the moon—the night falls, shedding itself
across my face. What kind of going out is this, the birds that pass
within the air, the grass, each departing through the circle of
the sun, leaving us, the night you are becoming mine? Nor can
I sense the air upon my back, knowing night alone as it begins

descending into me. What are we sure of now? It cannot be
the moon that turns within our grasp, but moons in metamorphosis,
or stars, but ages of the light that we shall never see. The place
that we are in is not between us anywhere, possessing no
position but the space through which our hands have passed, embracing night
where it comes down, a dance that does not issue from our bones, but from
strophes of the dark, eternities that turn within our flesh.

Toccata

We might have been asleep. All about us shadows fell across
our bodies, falling from the great trees beside us breathing in
the sun, the movement of the leaves playing on your face, and I
unable to discern your mouth and eyes. I think it is the moon
in memory, the trees exhaling through the shade reflections of
the moon. Nothing may be known but shadows as they fall, the sound
the sun makes passing through the trees and into air. It is

a spell to live so, remembering the moon gazing on
your face, thinking the stars, the trees standing up within
your breath, and where we thought the ground had been, a sky spread out
beside our hands. I lay my hand upon your back, a passage of
shade upon us both. Music rose up within the air: it is
not we who chant the world, but voluntaries of the sun that ring
forever through the darkness of our flesh and speak us into shade.

Implications

Autumn lay before us, the sun suspended over us in its
formalities. We did not walk, but knew our feet upon the grass,
how they moved and how the grass arose, a dance of infinite
proportion, seeing birds hovering within the air, the shape
of time asleep, and when their singing ceased, the air hung still
with song, the notes implicit in your face. It is a season of
adagios, and when I hear you speaking of the sun, the words

fall slowly into our ears, kneel there. I could not see
you any more, thinking it was the sun that filled my eyes, your voice
illuminating our air. If there is a paradise,
it is a moment when the sun is born, taking shape within
our flesh, a universe between us in our breathing in the sun,
no bird within the air that does not turn into our gaze, their songs
our sight assuming orbits, no moon too large for us to adumbrate.

Voice

I cannot tell you where your voice comes from, whether from the stars
or newly risen from the wind upon the sea, nor how your words
take shape within my body, forming things that I have never seen,
and where they move about, the sun a flaming rose and rooted in
my flesh. Sometimes in the silence that they leave my fingers touch,
and falling through them are abandoned gardens and their trees, the turns
the moon takes within the mind. I heard a sound among the trees

when all the birds had since departed. How does space begin to fill
but with annunciations of a primal light, the sun and planets
taking places in the air? There is no certainty of gods,
a cosmos floating in their hands. Call them, then, the dawn and us
their afternoons, answering divinity in twilight and
the moon become a garden in your breath. Only the trees appear
didactic in this light, their branches evocations of the air.

Apocalypse

We lay there, waiting for the light to happen. What would be the name
for what we know, the walls that held the room in which we lay dissolved,
no defence around us from the air that entered us? I think
the seeds of flowers and the trees will settle in our flesh and lie
with us. Is this how grass comes up within the dark to move
through the earth? We are a garden grown together, then, unable to
distinguish who was first to sense the rain, the light the moon distils,

falling on us both at once. When we are naked, lying side
by side—realities of grass the barest shape of what is known—
the transformations of mortality appear absolute,
the time that governs us directs the stars. Let the light happen
now when flowers in their essence stand on new horizons of our eyes,
the sun upon their leaves caressing us. What can we give the sun
but revelations of our flesh, bearing the light within our hands?

Sleeping

We fell asleep together, breathing in the same air. Nothing
rose within our dream and took the shape of birds, a tree and light
that fell astonished to the ground beside us where we lay beneath
the newness of the tree. I saw you sit and raise your hands into the air,
the moon arisen poised upon your finger tips. I do not know
if birds asleep would dream of other birds, but our dream is of ourselves,
and it is we who walk within ourselves asleep, the moon appearing from

your hand, and in the passage of the night the dead lie too within
the earth, the living lying on it, all in one embrace of earth,
and when we wake, roses will have taken root within our eyes,
our flesh the earth, the frailty of our bones engraved upon
the ground. We were not meant to see—being where roses are—
our knowing of ourselves the moon returning through the air we breathe,
and birds asleep within the tree, roses open to the moon.

Vigils

Morning did not appear within your eyes, it was your eyes, the sun
a rose and gazing on itself in flower. How shall I say to you
what being is or what the moon means, reflecting on the sea,
or stones you might have held within your hands? Inexorable are
the slowly passing nights. The trees are always where they stood beneath
the sun, their branches imperceptible against the sky. I feel
your body's weight against my own. What I know of you has gone

into the dark, your breathing keeping pace with mine. I think that we
are of the wind's calligraphy, the air forever shaping us
within our flesh. We never speak unless the earth, the sun and moon
assume us as their voices, even silence floating from our flesh.
The earth is breathing——: can it then be you I touch going ever through
the dark or is it earth revealed within my hands? Apocalypse
is everywhere. Roses utter it, your eyes, the stillest stone and night.

Departures

I saw you cry today and looked away. The light around your tears
did not stay still but broke, as each tear broke, and disappeared
within the mind. I could not see within them what I thought I saw—
the death of roses, friends who fall apart, gone again to ground.
The light that settled on us then could not be held. It was a light
of interstellar shape and age, and when it passed, clarity
fell beside us somewhere on the floor, as glass would fall perhaps,

without the pieces left behind or sound. You might have risen then,
replacing momentarily the light and how its passing felt,
alone within its absence, as if there were no cosmos just before
and only you and I were there. What can I tell you of the time
that passed between us then? It is a light possessing you and me
in one embrace, and when your hand goes forth to touch the sun, what else
does it obtain but us, a silence and the passing of the light?

Passages

Darkness had settled in your hair, and when it settled, I could see
its passage, everything absenting from my eyes. Should you ask,
I am not able anymore to say what form the trees took,
nor if there were clouds or galaxies, the rest. My knowledge is
of settling, its flowing down upon your face, and how I took
it in my hands. This is darkness, not descending but the pith
of our bones, an aspect of the moon that we forgot that floats

within the tides, within our breath. I thought the dark was everywhere
my fingers moved—your eyes the dark, your mouth. Should you speak,
the words would be the dark articulate within my ears, dark
anatomies that utter our shape. My fingers in the dark
have lost touch, their knowing not their own, the skin upon your face
upon my fingers too, nothing in between, and if the stars
should rise, their rising would be there, a punctuation of the flesh.

Waking

I remember birches standing near a house, and in the bright
air children's voices, other echoes through the leaves. Perhaps
they now have all become birds or melodies of birds that drift
through distant afternoons of air. Sometimes waking it cannot
be said what sun or moon is in the sky or where the sky might be,
but should you fall within my eyes, it could be said that then the skies
might burst, and heaven through its apologias of roses fall,

their petals strewn beside us where we lay, and in the dimness of
the light you thought they might have been a passage of the birds into
the silence of the air. But they were not birds, nothing more
than roses in their fall, a moment when the heavens open all
about us. In the rising of the sun I saw you as you may
have been, a ray of light that falls through dust, the birches and the air
to settle in my eyes. I think that memory is so—a rose

we thought to be a bird, and children we have never known, our hands
upon their hair that opens in the sun, their breath upon our skin,
children passing through a time where we have never walked. But when
you are before me, birches I have never seen take root, and I
upon their unfamiliarities of ground begin to walk,
every rose you may have held becoming mine, losing all
hypothesis, and who I was, turns day within your flesh.

Refractions

I stood beside your head and smelled the fragrance of your hair. It was
of autumn leaves, burning in the dusk, and birds before snow, unsure
of their departures. Now it is no longer fall, the light a sudden
stone that falls beneath the sun, and we begin to speak of autumns
we had known, the air in its tactility upon the lakes, and through
the naked trees children seen in passing, the flowers of our words
springing up invisible between us where we stood. What does

it mean to give you this, to speak of what we said again, to think
that this is where we are, the air alone in flower in the sun?
Last night I dreamt you were the moon and I the tides. Nowhere, then,
is where my being is but mirrored in its temporalities,
and when the light descends, its fall is multiple. When I look
at you, the knowledge of my seeing rests within my flesh, the stars
uttered there: water flowers floating back upon the seas.

Crows

Seven crows were sitting in a tree, each eye turned
toward the north. The wind was blowing through their eyes, the northern light,
auroras of the sun unravelling and intermittent in
the air, descending into seven crows, and all the light black,
the seven crows a candelabra naked underneath the sky
and sitting in a tree that grows in each of us. North
is where your weather is. I cannot see you any other place,

darkness descending, seven crows in silence, gazing on your bones.
You say you must possess the sky again, your hands going out
within the colder simulacra of the sun, the plenitudes
of space filling them and falling off. I cannot hand you more
than seven crows, a light that flickers out, the wind. And where will you
lie down within the night, what stars will turn against your head, bequeathed
to elements and air, and elegies within your mouth mute?

Rogation

We might have been together somewhere, sitting on a bench beneath
the sky, flowers perhaps in sight, a stream. I remember grass,
our feet beside each other, a sense of air, a bird that passes through
it and is gone, a song that settles in the grass that forms the mind.
I knew you from the sun. You wore it on your skin, the only clothes
that fit—but not the skin, earth it was and flowers opening
within the light, early flowers, red desire in the air,
and blue and yellow—colours that desire in its frailty

would take beneath the distance of the sky, unthinking of the stars.
How can I keep my hands from taking each of these flowers, bright
with its mortality, each a bird that we have heard somewhere in
the brevities of other springs forgotten with their skies and stars,
flowers, grass? Of my mortality I am certain now,
knowing it from that light your eyes shed, knowing it
from each flower standing in the garden of your flesh, and from

the memory of spring that moves between us, birds that are the mind
in sudden changes of the light. Where will I go, when I am not
beside you here, within what ground will I begin to walk, my mouth
going open into silence and the dark? The earth as we
have known it in the light is who we are outside. I bid you, earth,
to give us what you are, to take us home within the dark of root,
to lie in these beginnings of ourselves, mortalities exchanged.

Gifts

Bodies die. How then are we to celebrate the sun that feeds
upon our flesh? You gave me flowers. I gazed at them, standing in
a vase, and looked upon the world that lay beyond them, elsewhere through
the window. Trees were there, and any leaves I saw were leaves that I
remember, ghosts of leaves upon the branches, no season there
to speak about. But here are flowers. When you placed them in my hand,
I could not help but graze your skin. It's possible that solitude

takes root within the air that flows around our hands at moments when
the sun descends upon us. No one sees the light, you said, and we
within the light invisible are born unable to behold
ourselves. Consider flowers in the sun, the light becoming flesh.
The knowledge that we have is in our hands. It is not knowing but
the sun in flower, open in the light. We are unable now to move
but in rotation, hands in their incessance flowing into hands.

Clair de Lune

It was a time of roses, rain and night. More would be a rift
within the universe they were. Before roses open in
your hand, they float along the great tides, subject to the moon.
Their fragrance is of falling stars, nocturnal movements of immense
and solitary birds, reflected fire—sages dreaming of
themselves becoming spheres and turning with the sun. It was your hand
alone that opened underneath the moon, space taking shape
around it, every star unknown. If we could stand within the arc

that it describes, the fragrance of the moon within the night of roses
turning in your hand would open us, our bodies capable
of nothing but inhaling light, the seas, the undiscovered stars,
desire in ellipsis, the meaning of the moon made manifest
and moving through us, no gesture that we make the moon does not
possess. Sitting in the dark, the light is not oblation, it
is all that we can be, attar of roses raining in our flesh,
a distillation of our breath that speaks the moon in verse.

Obbligato

We lay together side by side upon the shore. It did not seem
the sea was what we saw, but aspects of eternity that rose
within our eyes, and when we breathed, it was the moon that moved our flesh,
a tide that rose and fell within our breath. I saw the gesture of
your hand, a wake within the air. The sky remained unchanged, the sand
beneath our bodies, trees that waited farther up the shore, and when
your hand returned to earth, the shade of what it made within the air

remained, and everything—the sky, the earth and trees—were turned toward
its passing, gravity that flowers from your hand. How can we rise
and walk away from ordinations of the air that clothe us so,
our flesh given up upon the shore? We thought we were but one
implication, you and I in interchange, oblivious
of moons that play upon us in the night, permitting us to be
music of our own in instants. We do not possess our hands:

they are but flowers handed over to the air. I touch them, they
are how music feels, their rhythms lunar, growing larger in
the night, feeding on the dark, no more opaque than what our skin
conceals. Music, then, hovering within the air, is all
we wear, and when our bodies move, it is in answer to the moon
radiant above the sea, no other immortality—
nor any shape of us engraved upon the shore—moving us.

Logos

The world was wet with rain. The light was not whole but broken through
the air. I heard your voice. It was not sound I heard, but nakedness,
a voice unclothed and passing through the air, becoming part of rain,
flowers in their early temporalities suffused beneath
your voice. I think that someday I shall be where lemons are in bloom,
the misty rain coming off the sea. There will be nothing in
the air to hear but flowers, distance and the light. While you spoke,

I was no longer sure of where I was, whose hand I saw before
my eyes, or why. Perhaps when we were spoken, the newness of our flesh
unadorned, we issued from a voice that never uttered word
before, and tissues of our flesh were woven from eternity
and its uncertainties. What is our reply but silence and
our flesh in its unravelling, orchards in their losing, light
in larger rays of their refractions spread in gusts across the sea?

Essai

Do not speak to me of seas, the music of the spheres: against
those pale eternities, I need your bones, the incommensurable
flesh upon your bones, the light that spreads across your body when
you move. But more than bones, the whiteness they possess, I want to see
you rise—another moon perhaps, illuminated from within
your flesh, turning in the air, music emanating from
your bones, rising in its mortality, your face forever turned

toward mine—and enter every word I speak, returning to the air.
Who knows what kind of music this would be, a music of itself,
music of bone that dwells alone within the dark, a summons and
completion? Now my speaking must become notation, gestures of
a music in its metamorphosis, measures that cannot
be sure of how their tempo shapes, possessed of dancing bones, of bones
that are the later moon, gibbous in my mouth and speaking bones.

Breath

I shall never understand the trees, and your sitting under
them, the stillness that they breathe of roses, rain. Perhaps
the trees are something we recall—their yielding absolute to sun
and rain, every weather written in their flesh—memory
becoming flesh. Is this why we touch each other through the dark,
to hold our weathers, taking in the rain, the smell of roses? If
I were to write your name, shaping letters through the night, I need

another alphabet, composed of roses and the fragrance of
a spring that rises intermittent through the mind, knowing the fall
of rain within my flesh, knowing the form of roses there—: it is
a language of subjunctive moods, the virtualities of rain
and rose becoming how you are in me pronounced, impossible
that any syllable should pass away, the breath that breathes the flesh
breathing you in alphabets of trees and rain and roses spelled.

Epigram

The lilac blossomed late this year. It was an afternoon of rain
and cloud, and through the afternoon I looked upon the flowers falling
white and purple in the air, inscribing rain. Finally you
have died, my friend. I am now the ground where lilac petals fall
purple and white, the silence that they are becoming mine, no need
to touch them as they pass to know their disappearance through the grass
and into earth, minuscule burdens of the afternoon set down.

Acacias

Shadows of the trees were moving on the walls, and somewhere near
children played. I saw you sitting there beneath the trees, beside
the wall, the sounds of children rising in the air. Perhaps I did
not see you then, but saw the sun—or not the sun, but what it yields,
the shape your body takes, composed of shadowed voices and the light
that interrupt the air, the whiteness of the wall behind. If the birds
of evening gather now, they would not seek their old towers but,

falling from the air of shaded afternoons, take their rest
somewhere near you sitting by the wall. Music, when we hear
it, seems to last forever, moving in us with the pace of suns,
shadows in its wake and sleeping birds, the air being rent
with children passing. Eternity is nowhere then but here—your hands
that fill with music overflowing in the air, and if we are,
it is the sun that in its setting is, and shade within your eyes.

Imago

On occasion in the night your face appears in silhouette
to me. It is your face in effigy, I thought, that I might see
but dare not touch, premonitory in its outline, all alone
and holding up the air that lay upon us. Nothing in the room
had changed, and yet the space that it contained made me think of trees
when they are old, and I could breathe the majesty that they exhaled.
I have read that elsewhere in the world, birds in their designs

are not the birds we think they are, but gifts that are conferred on us.
There were no birds within the room, only the memories of trees
spreading their roots in us whose seasons are uncounted in the end,
and only you and I, and images of dreams that come and go
among didactic trees. This was not sleep where we have been, nor can
we wake to our familiarities again, the birds that we
have known or trees, and words that I would choose to speak to you are now

not clear to me. Flesh cannot be what we are, nor can the things
that lie about us in this room respond to what we say they are.
They are in their simplicity the signs of some imperative
that we bestow upon ourselves, exchanging breath throughout the night
within the room where we have been. But what we are is so to be
unable, given to trees and traceries of birds. It is enough
that we have known the sun, the passages of night, the shape of breath.

Vocation

When we lie down at night, darkness lies upon us taking the shape
of us but in reverse, becoming our dark, and in us in
reflection what we dream assumes the lines of its going forth,
our bodies places where nocturnal air arises, exits of
the sun. Nothing that we know can be of flesh, and should we touch,
our hands unseeing grazing past themselves, what would it be within
the dark they feel but passage of the air, hands enfolding hands?
If we were ever found to lie asleep within the opening

of roses, eloquence and darkness would become the only country
where, lying down together, every word that we would speak
at home within the darkness of our voice, the exhalations of
the rose, would be the clothes we wear to make us visible. The dark
is not a shroud, it is the sound of breathing barely heard—then us
in our entire nakedness, the open rose of our calling
in the dark to where we are, the planets forming coronas
upon the words the dark interprets for us, lying so enrapt.

Parting

The light of afternoon, descending through the trees, rested on
your shoulder unaware until the sun had set. It might have been
a bird, waiting for evening to come, its disappearance in
the night, but it was not a bird, it was a passage of the sun
alone, nothing to touch, the knowledge of it evanescent. You
were standing in the passage, and there was no smile on your face,
merely birds in evocation, settling in my mind asleep,
and with you in the parting of the sun there was a rose that stood

in brevity and opened in your hand. O hear the birds how they sing
throughout the night, their song a breaking of the dark, the rose you hold
unsmiling and invisible, the light a bird that wakes within
the mind! The night in its beginning cannot be a severance of
the sun: it is the sun inverted, roses bursting in the shade
falling through your hand. I think that none can bear the beauty of
the world, and to see it is a breaking of the heart, the rose
through all the eschatologies of summer blown, your hand within the fire.

Moonrise

We never saw the moon so bright and full, and yet I could not tell
your body from the trees that rose about it, nor any animal
that pastured there. I knew it from the sounds that leaves will make when they
come back to mind. None of this will fall within our sight tomorrow
underneath the sun. The flowers will be new, and we will know
the trees, the animals, the fathomable air. The universe
at night is of the moon, its light a tide that rocks the planets, trees,
the animals and us in its embrace. We cannot move unless

the moon were moving too, the shadows that it casts a shadow shared.
When I touch your face, it is the trees I touch, the passing of
the animals, the night. So I touch the moon, the shade that grows
beneath its light. No moon moves in our embrace, it is
the tempo of our soul, measuring the night. We cannot grasp
more life than this, but to be alive is knowledge of mortality,
the moon aloft in us, and our being silence and the shade.

Harvest

I took the rose you gave me, plucking off its petals one by one,
and put the petals in a vase with other roses I had laid
to rest before. The breath of roses rises everywhere within
the room, and there is nothing not in some way coloured by their death
falling in the vase. I think that roses dream, and when they dream,
no one sees their dreams, but fragrances of what they dream begin
to dwell in us, nor can we put their petals anywhere without
their dreams disintegrating in us. We are then where roses dreaming

die. Is this a kind of sanctity, to walk within rosaria
of grace, no sound within our ears but petals falling? Roses die
perpetually, and we are vases of their immortality
where fragments lie of summers long forgotten and the sun, descended
from the sky and strewn upon the ground, no longer visible:
no other grief reposes in us so, garnering our death
before it comes, as if it were a rose undying where we are
to find ourselves more everlasting, the sun in pieces in our hands.

Rondel

Breezes came up at random, and ran through the flowers growing on
the fence. They would dance and then be still. You might have thought them bells,
the sounds they made transformed. We saw them from a window, flowers and
the sun behind them moving through the light embracing us. Music, perhaps,
begins within the sun, and planets, stars and moon in gravity
are poised, the music that is in them prompting flowers in their dance.
We held each other in the light—even flowers could not be

so fragile. Something in us moved, and if we were to hear them, then
we heard the air that flowered with the stars, a transmutation of
the sky moving into us. I cannot say whose hand it is
that touches yours, nor who it was that danced, thinking the flowers bells
or stars. What did I mean of roses and their brevity? The sun
in its eternity unfolds within us, roses opening,
and should we speak, the air around us would be heard to ring with stars.

Waiting

We lay surrendered to the rain. Antiquities of fish began
to rise within our bones. Around us in the trees without a sound
birds were moving in the trees. The only space we knew was shores
of sand and grass, the wind that passed beneath the trees. The emptiness
beyond we could not see, our flesh being nothing but a place
the rain filled, moving over lakes. The limits of my knowing
you are here. We wait for animals descending through the night,

their mouths about to drink, the silence culled from falling leaves. If we
are seen, it is the light that falls on us beneath the moon, the rain
for that occasion stilled, the shadows of the trees stretched out upon
the mirrored moon and us. We shall not rise from earth, waiting for
the rain to fall through trees and flesh and grass, the earth's divinity
the air that gives us shape. I cannot say you now, our faces turned
toward the heavens filling with the moon, its light our breath exhaled.

Absence

I woke within the night and thought that you had gone. Perhaps the moon
had fallen from the sky, nor was it space around us, only dark
and absence as a shelter over us. I could not hear you breathe—
no place within the universe to turn. It does not matter if
the sun will shine again, the curves of space unable to admit
divinity. Somewhere naked in the dark roses open. It
is solitude alone that flowers, nothing but the fragrance of

roses in their absence turning where the moon had been, the fall
of seas the silence of the open rose, your breath a rose exhaled.
Should I continue now to breathe for us, the dark would enter me,
memories of the moon, and certain knowledge of the rose that stood
beside us in the night, my bones assuming shapes of solitude,
roses in my blood, my breath in bloom, the darkness open and
in flower, firmaments of roses then respiring through our hands.

Zenith

I saw my mother yesterday, sitting in the garden, birds
around her head, and in her hand the yellow daffodils that I
had carried to her grave. Fearing I might startle her, I did
not move, my eyes on hers, and saw they were as if asleep, but not
asleep, and open to the circulation of the sun within
the air. I think the trees were leaning forward then to hear what she
might say, the daffodils within her hand appearing more alive
than if they grew against the ground. You are not mother now, I might

have said, if I had dared to speak, and saw your eyes turn upward to
the sun. Between your eyes and ardours of the sun there was no thing
that passed, the birds at rest. Never were your eyes so open as
they then appeared, taking in the sun, its majesty contained.
How can I speak of knowing you or now of knowing who I am,
the sun no longer in the sky? If we shall find eternity,
it will be memories of daffodils and hands that grasp the fire,
wherever your eyes gaze upon your glory as it turns in air.

Speaking

I spoke your name. The night gathered it in. I spoke your name again,
the echoes of its syllables becoming night in fragments in
my hands. Is this what speaking is, to take solitudes within
your hands, to feel their shapes before they turn again to silence and
the dark? I call you *rose*, the sound you are receding farther into
night until its memory is gone, the flowers that I saw
enfolding darkness in their blossoms, fragrances of stars and moon
upon my breath. I think it is not me who speaks, saying the rose,

its knowledge permeating air, but somewhere in me roses have
put down their roots, the fragments of my darkness holding them, and I
am night waiting for the flowering of stars. It is the night
alone that speaks, and when you stand beneath the moon, it is a rose
uttered there, the sound it makes becoming in the silence who
I am, the spring and mist before the dawn that rises from the fields.
Birds appear from nowhere, songs of roses fill it from their mouths.

Reply

We sat upon the ground, lying back to take the fullness of
the sun within our bodies, thinking summer over now. The trees
that gazed upon us were not trees but transformations of the sun
that stood more closely by, and silence fell upon us from the sky
absorbing us within the light. When we are death's possession, will
the sun be in us then, you asked from in the silence, bodies burnished
in the light, suspended through autumnal air and passage for
the undeparted birds? And what of sleep, when we are on the ground

oblivious, what memory possesses us, and what recalls
the grass that lies beneath us bent against the ground? I have but words
for you as my reply and where I think we lie, and sometimes light
descending from the sun is gathered there, the sun that's left in leaves,
turning golden in the passing of the year, and in the silence
of our bodies lying here, and shadows of the birds that spread
the dark in moments over us. I ask you then to take them as
they are—they hold us, each assuming our presence on the ground.

Of Roses

Someday in the end, when we lie undisturbed, a part of earth's
possession, and the trees are not within our sight but taking root
within the ground of what we were, nothing will be known of us
but words that are remembered here, words that once had grown between
us, words that took the shape of roses flowering against the snow,
of roses that I saw within your eyes, the ghosts of roses in
your mouth, the syllables in petals falling. As they fell, they spoke
of summer gone, and we became an elegy of roses for

ourselves, the snow coming down about us, silence visible.
Within the cage of bones we are, a rose stands up against the snow
proclaiming its eternity, the cadences of what it says
a tempo for our breath. Around the rose, the sun turns, the moon
appears, a universe in place, the undiscovered galaxies
waiting to become a word. I looked at you against the snow
and was not able in the light to see the shape you took. I know
your presence as an alphabet—: it spells the rose that says our name.

Palingenesis

If we are born again, what colour will the sky appear or where
will our ground be? Perhaps we will become stars or but
the light the stars shed, the smaller sisters of the moon, and if
we should be seen, what kind of story will we be, the figure that
we make suspended in the silence of the summer nights and both
of us becoming word, a genesis returning to itself?
Divinity is not beginning, it attends, and when we shall

be spoken, it shall waken, stars within the firmament, the moon
alive. We lie within each other's mouths, finding there the sky
and silence that contains whatever we would speak, the sleep of God
upon the grass and rising through the night, the space between our words
the silence open, things appearing, and of their mortality
no shade is cast, standing as they are within the light of stars,
no other shape against the air of our breath within the light.

Naked

When I speak with you, I have no certainty of what the words
will be, my mouth full of surprising trees, and part of me beneath
them lying with you in the sun, knowing you upon my breath—:
autumn is upon us, and we are left merely naked to the sun,
words falling in sudden gusts through our breath, nothing left
but trees and bones of thought, the seasons of abstraction stretched before
us, being visible. How can we think that what we say is ours,

the intimacy of our breath exposed, autumn in our mouth?
I hear you speak my name and know that I have woken, taking shape within
the air, your thinking of me now a revelation standing in
the sun, at home with trees, the seasons of finality. What are
we in our flesh but we as our particulars, waiting for
the sun to lay us bare, to find our bones in contemplation of
themselves, rapt in the sun, a universe anatomized in us?

Returned

I held your head within my hands. It might have been a fallen bird,
a stone, the moon in memory, but it was not a stone, and it
was warmer than any moon that passes through the sky at night
and then is gone. My hands are holding you, contemplatives of your
being in them, your speaking passing into flesh and bone, a word
incarnate and corpuscular. A time will come when I must take
my hands away, no longer made for grasping sense, and they will lie

somewhere underneath the moon, a stone for company, perhaps
a fallen bird. I think that sometime all that will remain of me
will be the silence of my hands, and when the trumpet sounds the final
time, my hands will clap once, and nothing will be heard but echoes
of all you said to me, no flesh put on again, but air alone
assuming sense——: the moon appealed to once, a stone, and memories
of birds aloft within eternal skies, both of us recalled.